Adventures

with

A String

BY HARRY MILGROM

Adventures with a String

FIRST SCIENCE EXPERIMENTS

BY HARRY MILGROM

Illustrated by Tom Funk

E. P. DUTTON & CO., INC.
NEW YORK

TO MY GRANDSON
Jerrold Scot Milgrom
and all the other inquisitive children
of his generation whose nimble minds
will help fathom more and more of the
unsolved mysteries of the universe
in which they dwell.

Published simultaneously in Canada by Clarke,
Irwin & Company Limited, Toronto and Vancouver

Library of Congress Catalog Card Number: 65-21287

Adventures with a String

A string is

an interesting thing.

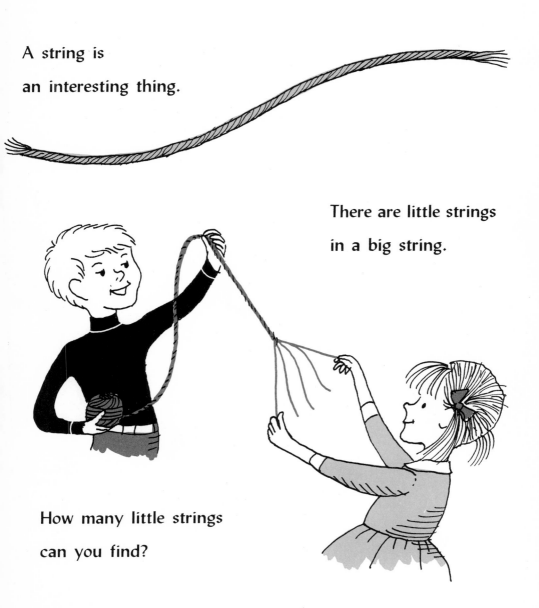

There are little strings

in a big string.

How many little strings

can you find?

Pull on the big string.

Pull on a little string.

Which string breaks first?

Why is the big string stronger?

Tie the string around two pieces
of wood.

Can you pull the pieces of wood
apart?

Tie the string to a toy car.

Pull the string.

What happens to the car?

Pull the string here –

– the car moves here.

Hold the string at one end.

Let it hang.

Does it hang straight?

Tie the other end of the string
to a heavy key.
Let the key hang.

Now

does

the

string

hang

straight?

The string hangs straight.

The key points down.

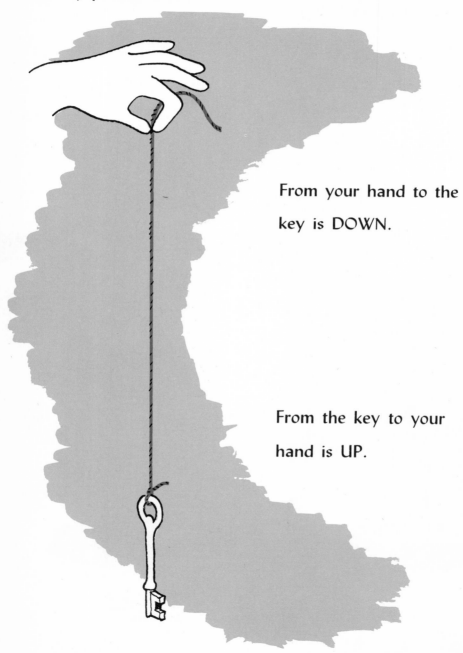

From your hand to the
key is DOWN.

From the key to your
hand is UP.

Twist the string in your hand.

What does the key do?

If you give the key a push,

what will it do?

It swings back and forth.

Make the string short.

Swing the key.

Make the string longer.

Swing the key.

Which time does the key swing faster?

Hang the string over a doorknob.

Pull the string down.

Which way does the key move?

When you pull DOWN

UP

goes

the

key!

The string changes DOWN to UP!

Wind the string around an empty spool.

Put a pencil in the spool.

Hold the pencil.

Pull the string.

What happens to the spool?

The spool turns.

A pull on the string makes

the spool go round and round.

The string changes a straight pull

into a turn.

Tie the string to a doorknob.

Let the string hang loosely.

Fold a piece of paper.

Put the paper on the string.

Pull the string hard.

What happens to the paper?

The paper flies up.

The string launches the paper.

Keep the string on the doorknob.

Pull it tight.

Snap the string with your finger.

What do you hear?

The string makes a sound!

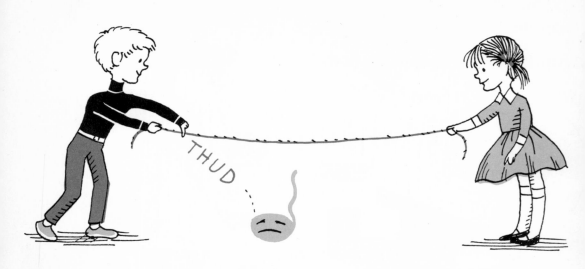

Hold the string loosely and snap it.

Hold the string tightly and snap it.

Which sound is higher?

The tight string makes a higher sound.

Snap the string when it is long.

Snap the string when it is short.

Which sound is lower?

The long string makes a lower sound.

The short string makes a higher sound.

Do you see why a string is an interesting thing

It holds things together.

It pulls things.

It shows which way is up.
It shows which way is down.

It twists things.

It swings things.

It turns things.

It throws things up.

It makes sounds.

What else can YOU
find out about a
string?

Think of what YOU
want to do.
Try it.

See what YOU can discover.